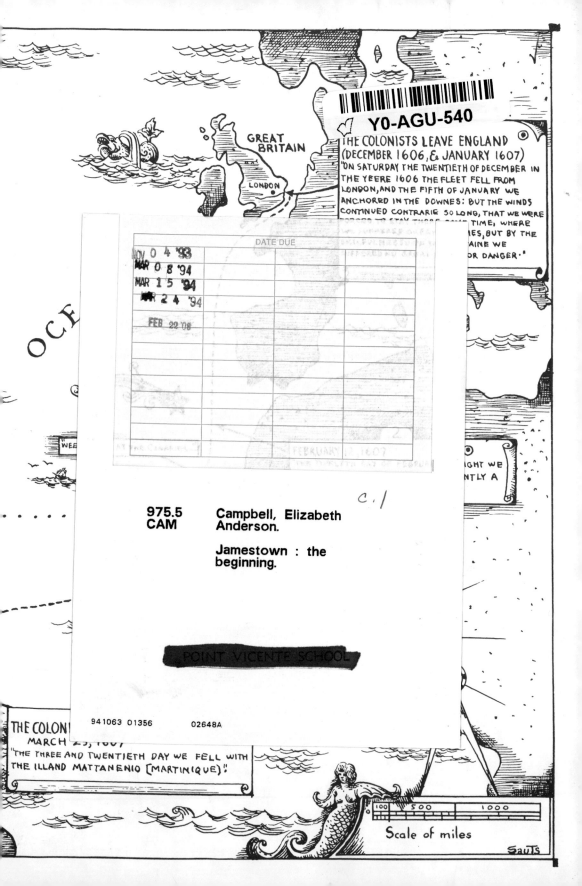

THE COLONISTS LEAVE ENGLAND
(DECEMBER 1606, & JANUARY 1607)
"ON SATURDAY THE TWENTIETH OF DECEMBER IN
THE YEERE 1606 THE FLEET FELL FROM
LONDON, AND THE FIFTH OF JANUARY WE
ANCHORED IN THE DOWNES: BUT THE WINDS
CONTINUED CONTRARIE SO LONG, THAT WE WERE

OR DANGER."

GREAT
BRITAIN

LONDON

OCE

THE COLON
    MARCH 23, 1607
"THE THREE AND TWENTIETH DAY WE FELL WITH
THE ILLAND MATTANENIO [MARTINIQUE]."

| 100 | 500 | | 1000 |

Scale of miles

SAUTS

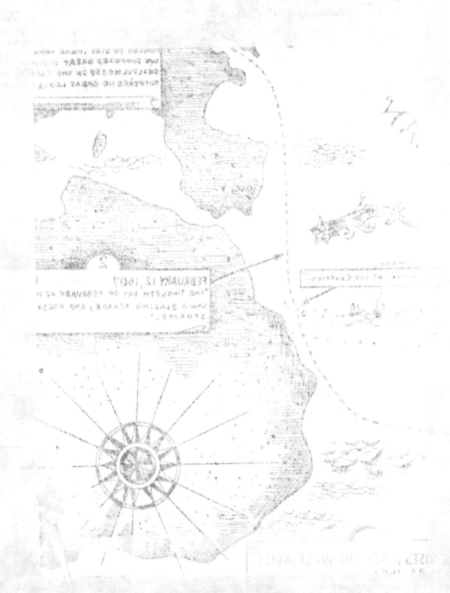

JAMESTOWN
THE BEGINNING

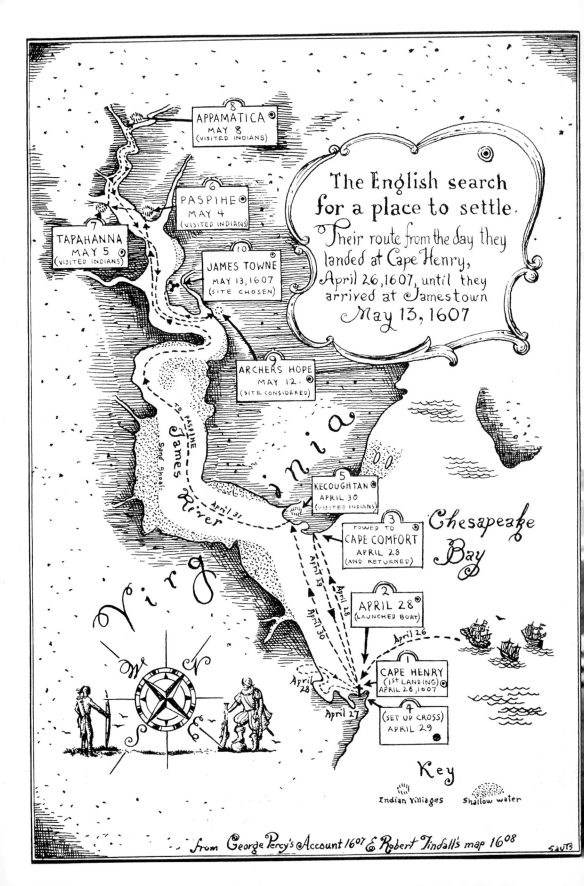

JAMESTOWN
THE BEGINNING

By Elizabeth A. Campbell

Illustrated by William Sauts Bock

LITTLE, BROWN AND COMPANY
BOSTON   TORONTO   LONDON

Books by Elizabeth A. Campbell

NAILS TO NICKELS
  The Story of American Coins Old and New

FINS AND TAILS
  A Story of a Strange Fish

THE CARVING ON THE TREE
  A True Account of America's First Mystery:
  The Lost Colony of Roanoke Island

JAMESTOWN: THE BEGINNING
  A True Account of the First Permanent
  English Colony in North America

The maps were originally drawn by Sidney E. King
for *A Pictorial History of Jamestown, Virginia* by
J. Paul Hudson, copyright © 1957 by J. Paul Hudson.
They were redrawn for this volume by William S. Bock.

Library of Congress Cataloging in Publication Data

Campbell, Elizabeth Anderson.
  Jamestown: the beginning.

  SUMMARY: Describes the founding of Jamestown, the
first permanent English settlement in North America.
  1. Jamestown, Va.--History--Juvenile literature.
[1. Jamestown, Va.--History] I. Bock, William Sauts,
1939-   illus. II. Title.
F234.J3C35   917.55'421   73-14652
ISBN 0-316-12599-7

BP

Published simultaneously in Canada

by Little, Brown & Company (Canada) Limited

PRINTED IN THE UNITED STATES OF AMERICA

For
our godchildren,
my unselfish husband and Mom,
whose encouragement and love
have made this story a reality

Acknowledgments

The author is grateful to J. Paul Hudson, Museum Curator–
Archeologist of Jamestown, Virginia; Charles E. Hatch, Re-
search Historian of the Historic Preservation Team–East; Dr.
Ben C. McCary, Professor of Modern Languages Emeritus,
College of William and Mary; and the National Park Service.

Britans, you stay too long,
Quickly aboard bestow you,
And with a merry Gale
Swell your stretch'd Sayle,
With Vowes as strong,
As the Winds that blow you.

. . .

And cheerfully at Sea,
Successe you still intice,
To get the Pearle and Gold,
And ours to hold,
VIRGINIA,
Earth's onely Paradise.

from "To the Virginian Voyage"
written by the English poet
Michael Drayton in 1606.

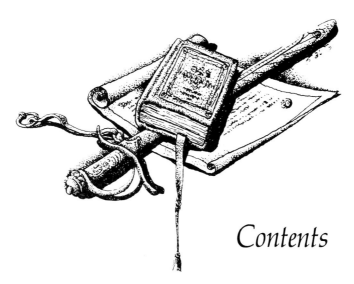

Contents

JAMESTOWN

THE BEGINNING

Plans

Many adventures begin with plans. Some plans are exciting and frightening; some call for a new and brave way of looking at the world.

Such plans led Christopher Columbus and his sailors to North America in the fifteenth century. They thought they had reached India, so they named the people in the new land "Indians."

In the sixteenth century other brave explorers from Europe planned and made trips across the Atlantic Ocean to the New World. The northern wilderness was claimed by France. Spain claimed the southern regions and sent a colony of men to live there and explore.

The English claimed the land in the middle, from the coast westward into the unknown. They named the land Virginia.

Sea Serpents and "Divils"

By the last part of the sixteenth century, only the bravest dared sail to the New World. Sailors told stories of scaly sea serpents with giant heads and glassy eyes. It was said the serpents could swallow sailing ships in one hungry gulp.

There were also stories about islands of "divils" where ghostly wailing could be heard. Mermaids, calling from rocky coasts, were said to have enchanted voyagers with magic songs of promise. Some ships never returned.

But, in spite of the scary stories and other dangers, a small group of daring Englishmen sailed to the New World. They were sent to select a site for a colony that would follow.

Landing on the unexplored coast of Virginia, they lived on an island among the Roanoke Indians, one of the Algonquian tribes.

After a few months the explorers returned to England with two Indian visitors. They had found a site for the first English colony in the New World.

The First Colonies

When spring came again, seven ships of Englishmen sailed to Roanoke Island.

At first the Indians there were friendly. They helped the Englishmen build an earthen fort for protection from the unfriendly Spaniards. The Indians planted corn for the English and taught them how to make fish traps.

As the Englishmen explored along the coast, one of their company, John White, drew maps and pictures of life among the Virginia Indians.

Before long, the first colonists tried to make the Indians obey English laws. One misunderstanding led to another. An Indian village was burned and soon friendly neighbors became enemies. The first colony was glad to return to England.

In the year of 1587, a second colony of men, women and children sailed to Virginia. They were afraid to settle on Roanoke Island and wanted to travel farther north near the Chesapeake Bay.

But the navigator refused to guide the ships past Roanoke Island, so the colonists repaired the wooden huts left over from the first colony and hoped for Indian friendship.

A girl was born within the colonists' earthen fort and named Virginia Dare. She was the first baby born

of English parents in the New World. Soon afterwards, her grandfather, Governor John White, returned to England for supplies.

During this time, Spain and England declared war with each other. The ships of England were kept close to home to guard her island shores.

Nearly three years passed before Governor White could return to Roanoke Island with supplies. When the Englishmen arrived there was no one on the beach to greet them. Hurriedly and fearfully, they stumbled through tangled vines to reach the fort.

But the houses were gone and the settlement was deserted. A few scattered belongings and rusty armor lay decaying in the weeds.

The second English colony in Virginia had disappeared, leaving only a word carved into a tree trunk— CROATOAN.

Hurriedly and hopefully John White urged the captains to sail toward Croatoan, an island near the Virginia coast where a tribe of Indians had lived.

But the winds of the Atlantic Ocean had other plans. A storm arose and the ships could not anchor near the island. Discouraged, the captains turned the sails toward England without having found the lost colony.

Indians

For several years Spain and England continued to wage war. The land of Virginia was almost forgotten.

At last, Spain signed a treaty of peace with England. It was an uneasy peace, but England was relieved.

A spirit of exploration began to sweep across the land again. Dreams of adventures and wealth made England's younger generation restless. Merchants were eager for wares that England could not produce. The poor farmers and tradesmen were looking for a way to make a better living. The ladies of King James's court wanted shiny silk dresses, soft furs and sparkling jewels.

One day some explorers returned from the coast of the New World with exciting visitors. Five tall Indians walked with them through the streets of London. Ornaments of copper, shell beads and pearls hung around their necks. The proud visitors seemed to be proof of friendly Indians in the New World.

A merchant of London soon called his friends together. "I have a daring plan in mind," he told them. "A plan that will require permission from the King."

Eastward, Ho

King James was delighted with the merchants' plan to send a new expedition to Virginia. Perhaps they would find a shorter trade route to the Orient, as well as silver, gold, and other treasure. He gave the men, who now called their group the Virginia Company of London, a "royal charter of permission."

The first task that faced the Company was to raise money for ships and supplies. A worthy sea captain had to be found to command the expedition. Adventurers had to be found to go along. Excitedly, the merchants began to advertise.

Hand-printed "broadsides" were posted in public places. "Invest your money in a Virginia colony," the advertising read. "Invest twelve pounds and ten shillings and you can be lord of 200 acres of land forever."

Speakers, writers and poets urged adventurers to go. They exaggerated and encouraged with stories of gold, silver and other treasures that might be found in Virginia. Ministers preached the joy of teaching Indians about a Christian God.

No one mentioned unfriendly Indians or Spaniards. Frightening stories about the "lost English colony" were forgotten.

"Off to Virginia!" was the cry. "Off to Virginia and hunt for GOLD!"

The Sailing

The year was 1606.

Three small ships sailed proudly down the Thames River from their anchorage at Blackwall. Awkward-looking and whale-like, they were twice as long as wide. Square linen sails curved skyward to catch the breeze.

Sailors on the deck of an anchored warship stopped polishing cannons to watch. They laughed at the slow, heavy ships passing the city of London. "Hoist yer anchors!" they yelled.

Heavy ships they were indeed, and difficult to steer. Yet many an angry sea had failed to swallow them.

No longer were they hauling coal from Russia in their holds. Today they boasted brightly decorated hulls and new names that showed faith and hope: *Susan Constant, Godspeed* and *Discovery.*

Aboard the ships were one hundred and five adventurers. Four were boys. The crew of thirty-nine sailors hoped to return to England someday. There

were soldiers, a blacksmith, a doctor, a minister, a drummer and nearly fifty listed as gentlemen.

Some gentlemen had never learned a trade or profession, nor earned a blister. They were happy and excited with visions of treasure in the new land. Doffing their plumed hats politely, they waved to the watchers on the banks of the Thames.

"Off to the New World!" an excited cabin boy yelled.

"Guard 'yer tongue, lad," snarled a soldier and gave him a face-burning slap. "The ears of Spain are everywhere. And the Spanish do not want Englishmen in the New World."

Captain Christopher Newport

Captain Christopher Newport stood proudly on the deck of his flagship, *Susan Constant*. The Virginia Company had chosen him to lead the expedition.

He had gone to sea when only a boy, and his life had been full of adventure. He was one of six Masters of the Royal Navy. At age forty-six, he was not yet an admiral, but he was respected as one.

Captain Newport leaned into the wind. His sturdy legs were planted firmly on the oaken deck.

His right sleeve was empty and pinned to the shoulder of his scarlet coat. His left sleeve was filled with a muscular arm, and his wind-tanned hand rested on the sword hilt at his side.

The warship anchored in the Thames brought back memories. Memories of sea battles for Spanish treasure, of pirates and gold. The captain's privateers had once captured nineteen vessels at one sweep, but a Spaniard had slashed off the captain's arm.

On a recent voyage he had pleased King James with strange animals he brought back from the West Indies: a crocodile and wild boar.

How different this new command would be! Three merchant ships filled with seed oats, barley and wheat. Besides food, they carried muskets, breastplates, gunpowder, tools, trade trinkets, bibles and prayer books for spiritual needs, and many other supplies.

The Virginia Company of London had given the captain "sole charge and command." It would be his duty to keep peace and health among tradesmen, laborers, soldiers and gentlemen as well as the crew.

Smokey December fog swirled around the small ships. The chimney pots of "London Towne" were lost to view. Boatswains' silver whistles called to each other in the grey mist.

Christopher Newport straightened his shoulders. His far-seeing eyes peered through the fog as he faced a destiny yet unknown.

The Sealed Box

The three ships sailed into the Atlantic Ocean from the Thames and southward down the English coast.

On the deck of the *Godspeed,* Reverend Robert Hunt bowed his head in prayer. He prayed for wisdom and guidance in helping so many ranks of men.

A lonely middle-aged soldier leaned over the rail of the *Godspeed.* The curling white breakers reminded Edward Wingfield of the ruffled nightcaps of his children. He wondered if he would ever see them again.

On the flagship, *Susan Constant,* Captain Newport was kneeling in front of his oak sea chest, behind a closed cabin door.

Inside the chest, under clothing and armor, sat a small wooden box. Carefully, the captain lifted out the box for examination. It was decorated with polished brass bands. A large splash of wax covered the latch. The seal of King James I was imprinted there.

The sealed box had been delivered to the dock at

Blackwall just before the ships had sailed. "Guard it carefully," the King's message said. "Open it the first night after landing in Virginia."

Stranded

Suddenly the boatswains' silver whistles sounded sharply and clearly.

Captain Newport quickly replaced the sealed box in his sea chest. Flinging open the cabin door, he looked down on passengers and crew. Their eyes were raised to the sky.

The flags of England and Scotland fluttered feebly from their masts. The red cross of Saint George no longer waved brave greetings to the sky. The sail-blowing winds had disappeared.

The small pinnace, *Discovery*, was hardly more than a fishing boat, twelve feet wide and three times as long. She bobbed up and down like a fishing cork, and most of her twenty-one passengers were already seasick. Pale and dim-eyed, they hung over the side. The contents of sick stomachs heaved into the sea.

Sea gulls circled above the bent heads. They seemed to screech in hoarse voices, "Stranded, stranded, stranded!"

Suddenly there were no winds at all. The ocean was flat and glassy, as before a storm. The ships were as helpless as three fat whales on a sandbar.

"Contrary winds, come back, come back," chanted the ship's boys.

Waiting

George Percy sat on a coil of rope with his knees for a desk. With his quill pen he was writing a daily record of the voyage, entitled *Observations*.

"On the fifth of January we anchored in the Downes," wrote the young soldier.

Nearby, Captain John Smith sat on a barrel of supplies and fished from the deck. He and George Percy had traveled in many lands and fought in the Low Countries of Europe. In the England of their day, warfare and foreign travel were a part of education. Now they were ready for adventure and riches.

A ship's boy leaned over the rail by John Smith's side.

"Why did we leave England five days before Christmas?" the boy asked the captain.

"The journey was planned in order to reach the New World by spring," he explained kindly. "Spring for planting, building and exploring. Good weather for the making of clapboards to send back to England."

"We will never reach Virginia by spring if the winds don't return soon," grumbled a gentleman named Edward Brookes. "Here we sit like sea gulls almost in sight of our own shores."

"Oh, be of good cheer," reproved John Smith, slapping him on the back. "Mariners and soldiers are accustomed to the will of the winds."

" 'Tis a bad beginning, mark me word," warned a peg-legged sailor as he spat into the sea.

The Decision

The ships rocked at anchor for nearly six weeks. Now four men sat in Captain Newport's cabin behind a closed door.

John Ratcliffe, captain of the *Discovery*, sat on the sea chest. "I fear mutiny on our hands," he growled, and slapped his scabbard as though expecting an attack at any minute.

"My scurvy crew tells tales of blood-thirsty cannibals and sea dragons which swallow ships," he continued. "We sleep in the foul-smelling hold together. Lately fights are as common as weevil in our gruel."

"We have already eaten six weeks' worth of rations that were meant for use in the New World," reminded Captain Gosnold of the *Godspeed*. "I fear starvation and spreading fevers. Reverend Hunt has been nigh unto death."

Captain Newport's keen eyes looked into the Reverend's pale face. "And what say you?" he asked.

" 'Tis true I have been ill along with others," answered Robert Hunt. "We have suffered wild storms and harsh words of discontent. But by God's will, we are yet alive. England needs a colony in Virginia. Let us wait and pray for the winds."

Christopher Newport's shoulders straightened. "My thanks to you," he said, rising. "Cut all rations to 'six upon four'. We will wait for the winds."

"Six Upon Four"

On the twelfth of February, a blazing star streaked across the heavens. Some of the men felt it was "a sign." Whether it was a good sign or bad, they did not know.

The rations of four men were now feeding six. The water casks were almost empty. There was a feeling of mutiny in the air.

The ragged sailors gathered by the rigging on the *Susan Constant*. Their battle-scarred bodies wore clothing of slain enemies from foreign ports. Fringes of matted hair stuck out from under knotted scarves. Their large, looped earrings jangled nervously.

"Six upon four," a one-eared sailor began to chant, and his mates joined in.

> "Six upon four. Six upon four.
> Bring a lad to the chest
> Or be cut even more."

Many sailors believed that a ship's boy must be whipped or "brought to the chest," to break a calm at sea.

The ship's boys tried to hide in the darkness of the

holds. Wide-eyed with terror, they cowered against the bulkheads, behind barrels of supplies.

Suddenly, as if by command, the winds came from the north. The ships rocked impatiently. Boatswains' whistles filled the air.

The sailors walked round and round, pushing the capstan bars to wind the anchors from the sea. Sails were pulled skyward. A deep-throated work chant rose from the crew. "Heave—ho! Heave—ho!" All thoughts of mutiny were forgotten for the moment.

The three ships at last set sail again—toward Virginia and the unknown.

Mutiny?

Near the coast of Africa, the Canary Islands were sighted. Anchoring offshore, the sailors eagerly rowed to land to refill the water casks.

Captain Newport knew that his adventurers needed fresh food, sunshine and exercise. Dysentery, scurvy, colds and coughs plagued the whole short-tempered lot. If fevers struck, it would not be uncommon to bury many men at sea.

Suddenly, the captain's thoughts were broken by

angry shouting. His cabin boy came running up the steps.

" 'Tis mutiny, sar!" he called as he pounded on the cabin door.

On deck, a short, red-haired soldier stood in the center of a shouting group. Above a curly beard, his high-browed face was flushed with anger. As he stood braced, with legs apart and sword drawn, no gentlemen dared challenge him.

Captain Newport hurriedly tried to recall stories about this young man, John Smith. He had heard that Smith gloried in strange lands and people. While a soldier, he had been captured by fierce Turks and sold into slavery. Killing his cruel master with a threshing bat, he had escaped home to England.

An experienced soldier would be needed in the New World, thought the captain. One with the self-confidence of this young man. Yet, it looked as if Captain Smith were trying to start a rebellion on the ship. Mutiny was a serious matter, and tempers were short.

Until a fair trial could be held, there was only one decision that seemed wise.

"Confine him below," commanded Captain Newport.

The harsh snapping of leg irons ended the day. Captain John Smith was a prisoner.

Cannibals?

The islands of the West Indies lay against the horizon like a broken necklace of green beads.

Captain Newport knew the islands well. Here he had fought Spaniards on land and sea, and lost his arm. Nearby he had captured the nineteen ships of Spanish treasure for England. Captain Newport decided these islands would be a fine place to exercise his men and to trade for food.

Naked islanders in canoes paddled swiftly toward the English ships from the beach at Dominico. Their tattooed, red-painted bodies glistened in the tropic sun. Dark hair braided in three plaits hung waist length behind their backs.

"They be cannibals!" hissed the peg-legged sailor. "Watch for their poisoned fishbone arrows. Take care or be meat for their stew."

The Englishmen jangled bells, beads and copper trinkets in the air. But trinkets were not unknown to these islanders. The ships of Spain and Portugal brought gifts, too. Beads and copper jewelry hung from their ears, noses, and lips and around their necks.

The canoes bumped against the ships' bowed sides. Mouth-watering smells of ripe bananas and pineapples tantalized the Englishmen's noses. In the canoes there were lemons, limes, potatoes and leather from wrecked Spanish ships.

The islanders climbed the rope ladders. The English gentlemen watched and waited, while the frightened sailors backed away. But before long, peaceful trading began on the decks.

The adventurers were beginning to sense the strange land they were entering.

Would the Indians of Virginia be like these? they wondered.

The Last Island

The ships sailed on with the next breeze. On the small island of Nevis, the men disembarked fully armed. Sentinels were posted while they hunted and fished. Their first baths since leaving England were enjoyed in the warm springs.

On and on they sailed, past St. Croix and Puerto Rico, to another island for more food. Wild pigs, sea tortoise, pelicans and parrots were carried to the ships. Although the men ate iguanas, George Percy called them loathsome beasts like crocodiles.

Many men fainted in the tropical heat, and one did not recover. Edward Brookes, gentleman, was buried on the island of Mona.

On April 9, the three ships entered the rocky shallows of a cove. "This is our last island," announced Captain Newport. "It is different from the others."

After the Englishmen had struggled up a steep mountain of sharp stones, an amazing sight met their eyes. A plateau of grass sheltered thousands of nesting birds. As thick as hail, they rose in deafening alarm and swooped over the intruders.

In three hours, the men had filled two boats with eggs, and two hogsheads were packed with birds.

The Englishmen had explored in and about fourteen islands in nineteen days. Now the prows turned northward toward Virginia—over 1,400 miles away.

Northward

Three wind-lashed ships rolled in a stormy sea. Two captains peered through the sheets of rain for the sight of their flagship.

A blazing torch of pitch burned on the swaying deck of the *Susan Constant*. Its flickering light was all that had kept the ships together through the nights of voyage.

" 'Tis four months 'ere we sailed from England. Where is this land Virginia?" muttered Captain Ratcliff on the *Discovery*.

" 'Tis four days we have found no bottom at a hundred fathoms," complained his helmsman, battling a single tiller.

Captain Gosnold peered into the darkness from the deck of the *Godspeed*. He worried about arriving in Virginia too late for planting time. The colony must have grains for winter gruel when left alone.

On the *Susan Constant*, Captain Newport's cabin door was closed. A flickering light showed through the cracks. He bent over his charts and maps, quadrant in hand, and studied them. The maps had been drawn by John White who had explored with the first Virginia colony over twenty years before. First he measured, then he looked at his mariner's compass and checked the sandglass for time.

Tempest or not, according to John White's maps and the captain's own navigation, they were right off the coast of Virginia. The brave captain propped his face in his hand and calmly waited for the light of day.

April Sunday

It was dawn on Sunday, April 26, 1607.

Most of the voyage-weary men were asleep. They lay below deck, curled among the nearly empty bags of grain. Sleeping lightly, they snored, twitched and dreamed.

Suddenly they were awakened by a cry, and they stumbled sleepily to their feet. A gentleman kicked over the cold iron cookpot as he ran. Hopping and holding his aching toes, he groaned, "What new danger now?"

The sailor in the crow's nest atop the mast was waving and pointing. "Land! Land, ho!" he cried.

The cries of "land" rang from ship to ship and seemed to echo from the shore. The mysterious shape of the New World lay just ahead.

The ships entered a broad bay. This was the Bay of the Chesapeake Indians marked on their maps. The "royal charter" for Virginia claimed 200 miles north and 200 miles south of the bay. It claimed 100 miles inland, too, though no one knew the actual width of the New World.

Everyone was excited and happy, especially Captain Newport. The helmsmen steered toward shore, and the adventurers prepared to land.

Some of the men unpacked heavy helmets and breast-plates. These were no longer used in English warfare, but they had been brought along to protect against Indian arrows. All of the men carried pistols or awkward, heavy matchlock and wheellock muskets.

By the time the sun rose, the small boats were ready to be lowered. The explorers paddled eagerly ashore and stepped onto a sandy, wave-flattened beach. They named their landing place Cape Henry for the son of King James I.

Englishmen were once again in Virginia.

Watchers in the Forest

The forest ahead seemed to reach out to the eager explorers. Live oak trees, wind-curved and ancient, hugged the sand dunes with gnarled limbs. Dogwood trees with white blossoms peeped from under sheltering pines. Walnut trees and hickories crowded together, their leaves overlapping.

When Captain Newport and his men explored deeper into the forest, they found meadows and fresh water in abundance. Raspberry and blackberry vines clung to the explorers' baggy breeches. Great ropes of grapevines climbed toward the sky, showing promise of juicy grapes.

Everything seemed to offer a welcome of spring.

What a "faire" and "goodly" land was Virginia! they all agreed.

The Chesapeake Indians had watched the ships with pale wings anchor in their bay. Now as the explorers entered the forest, the Indians were close behind. Barefoot and crouching low, they followed without being seen. Creeping closer and closer, they listened to the strange-sounding tongue.

Around winter campfires, the Indians had listened to stories told by their old priests. They knew of the ones with metal-covered heads who had landed before. Some had sailed away, and others had been sent to their *okees,* or gods, by Indian arrows. They had been *marrapough* (enemies), instead of *netoppew* (friends), the old priests said.

Now they had come again and had to be frightened away. The Chesapeake Indians sharpened their stone arrow points and waited.

Unwelcome

Captain Newport and his men marched out of the forest. Talking in loud, excited voices, they tramped bayward through dunes of waving sea oats. Their muskets were held at ease.

Suddenly, an eerie war-cry rose from the dunes. "I—e—ya! I—e—ya!"

Moving figures parted the sea oats. The surprised Englishmen turned around in disbelief. Fearfully, they tried to light the powder in their heavy matchlock muskets.

The sailors dashed toward the beached boats. Gentlemen lurched and stumbled in awkward breastplates.

The crouching Indians rose. How tall they were!

How short the Englishmen felt! Never had they seen people like these.

A loose knot of shiny black hair stuck out from one side of each Indian's head. Hair on the other side was cropped close to the skull. Skin quivers of arrows hung behind their backs.

By this time, the gunpowder had ignited. Thundering English muskets roared in billows of smoke.

When the air cleared, blood dripped from Gabriel Archer's hands. A sailor lay gasping from an arrow in his chest.

Frightened by the thundering firearms, the Indians had fled to the forest.

The peace of the sunny April morning was gone.

The First Evening in Virginia

The last rays of sun dropped behind the horizon. The fright of the afternoon was almost forgotten by everyone except the wounded.

This first evening in Virginia promised to be an exciting one. Captain Newport had asked the adventurers to meet on the *Susan Constant*. "There will be news of interest to all," he had said.

When the men gathered on the deck of their flagship, they learned that seven of them had been chosen

by King James to govern the colony. Which seven? they wondered.

Coins clinked as wagers were made. The men laughed, for if wagers were lost, it did not matter. Where could English money be spent in the strange New World? Besides, everyone would be rich when gold was found.

Some men leaned against the bulkheads. Others sat on the crowded deck with knees drawn close to their bodies. Every face was turned toward Captain Newport's cabin—every face but one. John Smith was still confined in the hold.

Christopher Newport stood on the high quarter-deck. His empty sleeve was tucked neatly into the velvet pocket of his best coat. Next to him, the cabin boy held a small wooden chest decorated with brass bands.

In one quick motion, Captain Newport broke the seal of King James from the lock with his sword. Hinges squeaked, as the lid rose slowly.

The captain lifted out a thick scroll, which the cabin boy untied and handed back to him. "These are our instructions," Christopher Newport announced, and began to read.

Instructions

The first instruction was to choose a settlement site. It was to be far enough inland to be hidden from Spanish ships. It was to be land of fertile soil beside a deep river.

After landing, they were to divide into groups. One group was to build a fort and a storehouse for supplies. Another was to clear land and prepare it for planting. The third group was to explore with Captain Newport, in search of treasure and a trade route to the South Sea of the Orient.

The scroll unrolled as the Captain read on: ". . . search for the 'lost colony' of twenty years before . . . teach the Indians about the Christian God . . . raise or trade for fruits and furs, cotton and cane, plants and herbs, lumber and tar, copper, silver, gold and precious gems . . ."

The gentlemen frowned and scuffled their feet. It was a tiresome list. They wanted to know which seven among them would be Councilors of the colony.

Captain Newport finished the instructions and cleared his throat. "Now for the Councilors," he began. "Edward Wingfield, Master; George Kendall, George

Martin, Mariners; Bartholomew Gosnold, John Rat-cliffe, Christopher Newport, Captains."

Captain Newport hesitated and looked closely at the scroll. The listeners stirred impatiently. "John Smith, Captain," he finished.

Quickly, Reverend Hunt stepped forward. Raising his hands for silence, he closed the meeting with a prayer.

The King's box was empty.

The Second Day in Virginia

The second day was beginning. Captain Newport and his explorers awoke early and armed themselves. They rowed back to Cape Henry to explore inland.

The Chesapeake Indians were also up and about early this April morning. They were feeding dead branches to a bonfire on the beach.

Some of the Indians pried oysters from their shallow river beds. Others placed the shellfish around the outer edges of the bonfire.

Hiss! Pop! Crack! Tiny bits of shell flew like arrows in all directions. The Chesapeake Indians blew on their burned fingers and ate noisily. They wiped the dripping juice from their beardless chins with the backs of their hands.

Suddenly, the sound of English voices reached their ears. Hurriedly dropping their breakfast, the Indians slipped quietly into the waiting forest.

Captain Newport's explorers had seen the smoke from the bonfire and curiously followed it. Their heavy armor clanked and creaked as they tried to hurry along the beach.

Muskets were lifted in preparation for an attack. But when they arrived at the bonfire, it was deserted —except for the steaming oysters.

The explorers were surprised and pleased to find a waiting treat. Taking turns standing guard, they ate the hot, juicy shellfish.

The Chesapeake Indians crept closer and watched from behind the sand dunes as their breakfast disappeared. Then, with angry mutterings, they hurried to warn the villages.

Off in the Shallop

While Captain Newport and his men explored on Cape Henry, the beat of hammers filled the air around the deck of the *Susan Constant*. The carpenters were busily building a flat-bottomed boat called a shallop, designed to move through the shallow water.

On the third day in Virginia, the Englishmen launched the shallop. Captain Newport decided to explore the cape on the opposite side of the bay.

When they landed, the Englishmen gathered mussels and oysters that lay clustered in thick piles near the beach. Some men found pearls in the oysters' soft stomachs.

In a field nearby they found an Indian boat about forty-five feet long. It had been made by scraping out and burning the inside of a tree trunk. The people of the West Indies had called this kind of boat a *canoa,* or canoe.

Marching inland, the explorers saw smoke. Venturing closer, they smelled burning grass. They thought it might be the Indians' way of clearing land. But then again it might be a signal for attack. Captain Newport decided to turn back his men.

As the men tramped bayward, they grabbed hungrily for wild strawberries. George Percy declared they were four times bigger and sweeter than those in England. They named the point of land Cape Comfort.

On returning to the ships, Reverend Hunt reminded the adventurers that they should thank God for a safe journey, and declared a prayer service.

The four carpenters hurriedly began work on a wooden cross. Early the next morning all the men rowed to Cape Henry, their first landing site.

While sentinels kept watch, Reverend Hunt bowed his head and prayed: ". . . to serve and fear God, the Giver of all Goodness, for every plantation which our Heavenly Father hath not planted shall be rooted out."

A cross was planted in the sand of Cape Henry. Then the ships sailed inland up a wide river, which emptied into the bay. The Englishmen named the river James, in honor of their king.

Meeting the Kecoughtan Indians

As the ships neared Cape Comfort, the explorers spotted Indians on the beach. Rowing shoreward in the scallop, the Englishmen smiled, each placing his hand over his heart.

In answer to these signs of peace, some Indians laid down their long bows. "Kecoughtan," they called. "Kecoughtan, *netoppew* (friends)."

Some Indians swam up to the shallop, holding their bows between strong teeth. Dangling earrings of birds' legs dipped in the water as they swam. Red and white streaks of paint decorated their shoulders. Their hands beckoned the visitors ashore.

On the beach the English and the Indians looked at each other with curious eyes. The Indians bent low toward the sand, bowing a welcome. Fringed deerskin pouches hung from every belt.

The Kecoughtan Indians led the visitors to a village where they were invited to sit on woven grass mats. The Indian men sat in a circle with the English.

The women moved shyly and gracefully among

their strange-looking guests. Some wore their coal-black hair in long, single braids. The younger girls had the front and sides of their hair cropped short. Apron-like skirts of fringed deerskin swayed with their bending bodies. Tattoos of painted birds and flowers decorated their bare legs and shoulders.

They served broiled fish, boiled hominy and strawberries. After the meal, the *werowance,* or ruler, passed around long stemmed pipes of tobacco.

Suddenly, the Indians jumped from their mats. Captain Newport's men raised their muskets in alarm.

The Dance

The Indians began forming a circle around a tall warrior. He began to chant and clap his hands. Bending forward, the others began circling and shaking rattles made of dried gourds. Heads, hands and bodies took up the rhythm.

Stamp, stamp, stamp-stamp-stamp. Voices rose and fell in a wailing chant. Bird-leg earrings swung as if in flight.

The dancers wore breechclouts of animal skins between their thighs. Animal heads hung from their belts. As they swung to the rhythm, the heads beat against the dancers' legs. The dried eyes almost seemed to stare at the Englishmen.

Suddenly, the whirling dancers stopped and looked at their guests.

Startled, Captain Newport dropped tiny glass beads and shiny pins into the hands of the Indians. Hurriedly the explorers said farewell and returned to the shallop.

Was the dance an unfriendly warning? they wondered.

Up the James

After four days of sailing up the James River, a small village was seen near shore. Happily, the Englishmen rowed landward, expecting another welcome.

But the Indians met them with scowling faces. The *werowance* made a long, angry-sounding speech. He called himself Wowinchopunck and waved his arms toward his tribe. "Paspahegh!" he shouted. "Paspahegh!"

The next day still farther up the river, the lookouts saw Indians waving from the shore. It was a relief to see a friendly tribe again.

"Tappahannock, Tappahannock," they called in excited voices. Gathering behind their *werowance,* they greeted the explorers on the beach.

How strange the fully-clothed creatures seemed to the Indians! What pale, hairy faces and iron-covered heads! And what straight, heavy-looking bows they held before them! But where were their arrows? The Tappahannock crept closer in curiosity.

The *werowance* played on his reed flute to welcome the visitors. A crown of deer's fur dyed red was fastened around a knot of hair on one side of his head. Two long feathers stuck out from the middle of the crown. A piece of shiny copper hung over the cropped hair on the other side.

The Englishmen tried not to stare too hard as they walked toward him. Little specks of silvery dust clung to his blue face paint. Bird-leg earrings decorated with copper and pearls swayed as he walked. A chain of shell beads hung over his red-painted body.

Captain Newport's men were filled with excitement.

They saw the pearls and the silvery dust and—was the shiny metal *gold*?

Leaving shiny blue beads, they hurried to tell their companions what they had seen.

Searching

The ships sailed close together in the May morning. Three more days had passed during which the English had explored even farther up the James. George Percy sat on a water cask and recorded his daily *Observations*.

"The Indians of Appomattock were not friendly," he wrote. "They carried heavy wooden swords set with sharp stones. Captain Newport has decided to turn back down the James."

Now the ships were anchoring off a point of land. George Percy put away his goose quill pen and joined the men who were going ashore.

Wild turkeys gobbled to their mates as the noisy strangers landed. Rabbits and squirrels scurried through the underbrush. The men saw an opossum for the first time and thought it was a monkey. Grapevines, each as thick as a man's thigh, hugged the trees.

Gabriel Archer hoped this point of land would be

their settlement site. Others felt the same, so they named it Archer's Hope.

"No," advised the mariners. "The river is too shallow here for ships to anchor by the shore. We need a fort site where ships can load and unload supplies."

"And we must have the ships' guns for protection while a fort is being built," added a soldier.

Captain Newport agreed, and remembered some low-lying land upriver which they had passed twice. It had appeared to be an island. Perhaps it was worth exploring.

"Swing the tillers, helmsmen. Hoist the sails."

Choosing

It was May 13, 1607, a day to remember in years to come. Late in the evening, anchors dropped through six fathoms of water into river mud.

Cypress trees spread their leafy arms over the tidal river. Mooring ropes of twisted hemp were tied to their thick trunks. The ships bobbed gently, resting water-soaked wooden bones. The weary Englishmen slept with dreams of tomorrow.

The worried Paspahegh warriors crept closer and

closer with arrows fixed in their bows. "They are *marrapough* (enemy)," their *werowance* had said. "Attack the pale-winged boats before it is too late," he commanded.

Near midnight, an English sentinel saw movement

in the underbrush beside the ships. Firing his musket, he raised the alarm. Unseen, the Indians slipped into the marshes to watch and wait.

When morning came, the eager men began to explore. The point where they had landed appeared to be an island at high tide, but at low tide an isthmus joined it to the mainland beyond.

Wild flowers bloomed in the woodlands. Timid deer bounded through the underbrush. Red-winged blackbirds sang cheerful songs as they swung on the marsh reeds.

The carpet of grass was comfortable to walk on. There were no farmers among them to notice any of the poor soil or the lack of fresh water. No one heard the whining mosquitoes in the acres of marshland— disease-spreading pests that would feast on the blood of the Englishmen in days to come.

The explorers begged Captain Newport to search no farther. Here they were ready to begin their dreams of Virginia.

They named the island "Jamestowne" (called Jamestown today) for King James I of England, thousands of miles away. Without knowing it, the colonists had chosen the hunting ground of the Paspahegh Indians.

Beware, Englishmen, beware!

Prayer Books and Axes

The first day in Jamestown was a busy one.

Land had to be cleared as soon as possible and prepared for planting. A fort had to be built for protection while the ships were gone. The Spanish had explored the coast long ago. The colonists feared Spanish ships might sail up the wide river again.

Reverend Hunt held a church service under an old sailcloth. A bar of wood was fastened between two trees for an altar, and the men gathered before it. The ragged, wind-torn sail kept the morning sun out of the chaplain's eyes.

Next, a Council meeting was held. Edward Wing-

field was chosen president. His troubles were just beginning, for there would be only four Councilors left
behind to help him when the ships returned to England for supplies.

John Smith's trial came next. First, he explained
that soldiering had taught him to act and react quickly.
Then, he declared that what he had said in anger on
the ship was never intended to be mutiny. Finally, he
reminded the group that he had an investment in the
colony, too.

The jury awarded Captain John Smith 100 pounds
of English money for the injustice he had suffered.
But they told him he would have to prove his worth
before becoming a member of the Council. "Use my
100 pounds for the good of the colony," said the short,
brave soldier. "I will prove my worth."

"Now falleth every man to worke," one colonist
recorded. Branches were cut and piled in a barricade
shaped like a half-moon. Behind the leafy fence, the
tents were propped and kettles were hung. Work on
a palisaded fort began.

The Paspahegh hunters listened to the thunder of
falling trees. They watched the frightened deer flee
across the isthmus to the mainland.

Something must be done!

Exploring

The first week passed quickly. On May 20, Captain Newport called a meeting on the *Susan Constant*.

"Two months were planned for me to explore," he began. "Now only two weeks remain 'ere I return to England. That is little time to search for treasure and the South Sea. Yet if the New World is narrow as mariners believe, we may still find a passage through it."

A babble of voices clamored to be heard. "We do not want to explore now. The task is impossible in so short a time," said many. "We are tired of rocking decks and unfriendly Indians. We are needed on James-town island." The protests fell like rain.

It was true that the Virginia Company of London was expecting a cargo of clapboards, or thin wooden planks, from the New World. There was little time left to prepare it.

Besides, Captain Newport's sole command at sea was over. The adventurers thought of themselves as colonists now.

But the Captain and many others knew the King's instructions should be obeyed. Bartholomew Gosnold stayed behind with President Wingfield to help govern

the contrary colonists who chose to remain at Jamestown.

Twenty-four explorers loaded the shallop. They
brought the usual trade trinkets, weapons, armor and a
small supply of food.

Four boys with sticks and an empty kettle stood near
the drummer. They waited to cheer their captain with
a noisy send-off. Perhaps he would find them a treasure,
too.

Our Island

At the first drum beat, the forest seemed to explode.
Before the explorers could shove off, Paspahegh Indians had swarmed into the encampment.

Curiously they looked into tents, tasted gruel, and
tried on helmets. There were cries of laughter, wonder
and desire.

The colonists had been instructed to keep all weapons from the Indians. When one Indian picked up an
English musket, a frightened colonist grabbed it out
of his hands.

The *werowance* Wowinchopunck shouted a command and the hunters rushed to the side of their leader.

Their faces became serious and hostile. How rude and selfish these pale-faced intruders were!

Angrily and desperately, Wowinchopunck tried to communicate. He scowled, pointed, shouted and waved his arms.

"You are building your houses on Paspahegh hunting land. Our deer are running away. Wahonsonacock, the Powhatan, the ruler of all our Algonquian tribes, said we must hunt here. We dare obey only Wahonsonacock."

"Wahonsonacock, the Powhatan, the Powhatan," shouted the warriors and raised their bows.

The colonists understood that the Paspahegh Indians were angry. They also realized that Powhatan was a powerful name among the Indians. But they did not understand that Wahonsonacock was the greatest of the Algonquian leaders. nor little else that Wowinchopunck told them. They shook their heads in bewilderment.

Wowinchopunck and his hunters pushed their

hidden dugout canoes from the marshes. With disgusted mutterings, they paddled upriver to their nearby village.

It seemed the strange ones could understand only the tongues of arrows. The Indians would wait and see.

To Find the South Sea

The explorers left the encampment and by nightfall they were miles upriver, past the Paspahegh villages. Gabriel Archer named places and drew maps. George Percy described the scenery in his journal. John Smith stored memories in order to write a history one day.

The next day the explorers approached an island. Wild turkeys gobbled in the forest, promising fresh fowl for the cookpot. A dugout canoe of waving Indians seemed to promise friendship. The explorers

decided to land, naming the island Turkey Isle.

Immediately, Captain Newport began trying to communicate with the Indians. "Where does the river go?" he asked.

One of the young Indians named Navirans understood. Using his bare foot he drew a sand map of the James River.

Gabriel Archer brought parchment and his goose-feather pen. Sitting cross-legged on the beach, Navirans drew another map of the river, showing rocky falls and mountains beyond.

Eagerly, Captain Newport asked what was beyond the mountains. *"Suckahanna,"* answered Navirans, and touched the water to explain.

"If water is beyond the mountains, it could be the South Sea," exclaimed Captain Newport. Eagerly, he invited Navirans to be their guide.

A few miles upriver, Navirans took the explorers ashore to a large village. After a feast and dance of welcome, a tall Indian visitor appeared. Two shouts of greeting filled the air, and Navirans announced "Parahunt, the Powhatan."

The Englishmen remembered the name Powhatan and wondered if this man Parahunt was ruler of all the Algonquian tribes. Captain Newport thought it wise to present him with beads and copper.

Parahunt accepted the gifts with great dignity. He invited the Englishmen to come upriver to his village, and they eagerly followed him.

Captain Newport's Feast

In Parahunt's village, Navirans showed the people his beautiful map and goosefeather pen. Parahunt understood that the visitors wanted to explore. He loaned the Englishmen six strong warriors as guides.

To show his good faith, Captain Newport left one terrified sailor as hostage until he returned. "On to the falls, the mountains and the South Sea," the captain commanded joyfully.

The sailors rowed Captain Newport, his Indian guides and a few other English explorers upriver. They labored through shallow water for about three miles. There the Englishmen saw the rippling rocky falls where the tidal James River ends. Captain Newport knew that only an overland march could take anyone farther.

"I have not given up," he declared. "We must explore on foot beyond The Falls. But now let us turn again down river to Parahunt's village."

The next morning everyone was busy on the shallop.

Captain Newport had decided to ask Parahunt for guides to lead the explorers on an overland march beyond The Falls. But first he would invite the *werowance* to a feast on the beach.

An iron cookpot was filled with salt pork and dried peas. Then beer and Spanish wine were carefully packed. Navirans hurried ashore to extend the invitation.

Soon Parahunt and his men were rolling unfamiliar food and drink over their tongues. Their throats tingled and their stomachs burned from Spanish wine. Licking their salty lips, they talked loudly, waving their arms, now laughing, now scowling. Only Navirans understood what they thought of English food.

The explorers asked many questions about metals, precious stones, mountains and rivers. Parahunt promised Captain Newport to meet him later at The Falls.

Hurriedly the Englishmen prepared for the overland march. How wonderful it would be to find the South Sea!

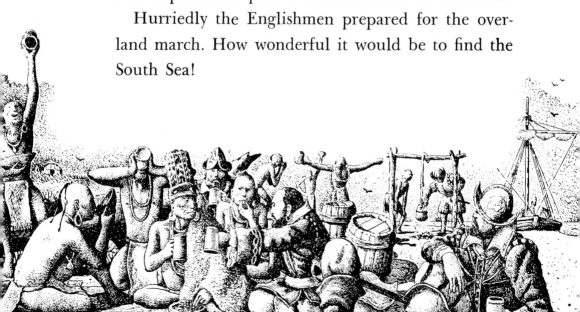

The Refusal

That afternoon at The Falls Parahunt and his guides came striding out of the forest. Navirans gave two shouts of welcome, and the meeting began.

Parahunt refused guides for inland exploration and tried to explain his refusal. The falls of the river were near enemy territory. The Monocan-Sioux Indians lived less than a day's march away. Parahunt said they were *maskapow,* meaning the worst of enemies.

In desperation, Captain Newport made a wild promise. He said he would send Parahunt hundreds of soldiers to fight his enemies. An army in exchange for guides!

Parahunt's face showed embarrassment and beginning anger. I can fight my own battles without help from this one-armed stranger, he thought to himself. I am a great warrior, son of Wahonsonacock, the Powhatan, the ruler of all our tribes. I have given friendship. Is this not enough?

Turning quickly, Parahunt stalked into the forest. His guards followed. Their faces were as stormy-looking as the darkening sky.

The discouraged Englishmen fashioned a wooden cross. Into the crossbar they carved the words

JACOBUS REX (King James). Captain Newport carved his name in smaller letters below.

Setting the cross in the rocky shallows at the foot of The Falls, they knelt in prayer.

Navirans was puzzled and frightened. There were many things he did not understand.

"Opechancanough," he whispered to himself. "Opechancanough will understand."

Navirans Leads

The shallop moved swiftly downriver once again. One defeat did not mean another, the explorers reasoned. They had not yet discovered where the Indians got copper, silver and gold. Visiting more villages might yield the answer.

A hurried stop was made at Parahunt's village to present him with a hatchet and coat. He seemed to accept the gifts as an apology. The Indians of his tribe appeared friendly once again and waved deerskins in farewell.

Back in Navirans's village, the explorers rested. They learned about a poison for Indian arrowheads called *wisacan*. They ate ground corn which had been formed into balls, boiled, then sun-dried on a stone.

Navirans began rushing the Englishmen on. He smiled secretly, but he would say nothing. Anchoring the shallop at the mouth of a small river, he led the curious explorers ashore once again. Captain Newport hoped that they were being guided to visit Powhatan, ruler of all the Algonquian tribes.

The explorers trudged through fields of growing corn. In the center of each cornfield was a covered platform supported by tall poles. On each platform, an old Indian or a child squatted hidden and silent, protecting the grain from hungry animals.

Farther on, the explorers entered a village. Many young Indians were busily flaking stones and animal bones into arrowheads and tools. Tiny, black-eyed babies swung from cradleboards on their mothers' shoulders.

"Come," urged Navirans. "Come." He moved

proudly, accepting admiring glances from the maidens nearby. His pace slowed as they reached a large house. Tall, unsmiling guards stood on each side of the rolled grass mats which hung over the door.

Navirans spoke a soft greeting and motioned for Captain Newport to enter with his men.

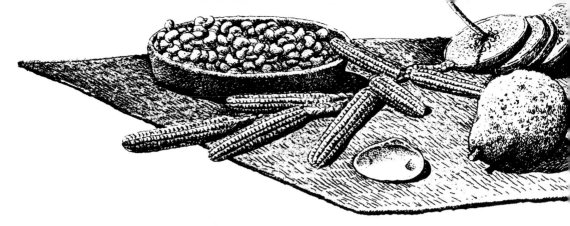

Opechancanough

Inside the cool dwelling a stern *werowance* sat on a pile of furs. A heavy-looking copper ornament encircled his neck. His face showed neither curiosity nor welcome.

Tall warriors formed a semi-circle behind the ruler. A young maiden placed a cornhusk basket of strawberries at his feet.

This man was Opechancanough, ruler of over one thousand Pamunkey Indians. He was visiting in the village, and Navirans had brought his new friends to meet the great *werowance*.

Suddenly, Captain Newport began to hope again. Perhaps this powerful man would offer guides to lead his explorers beyond The Falls.

Because time was growing short, Captain Newport did not offer gifts nor food. He asked Navirans to tell Opechancanough about their visit to Parahunt and to ask for guides.

As Navirans spoke, Opechancanough's unsmiling face became a storm cloud. "How dare they visit Parahunt first? I am the brother of Wahonsonacock, the Powhatan. Brothers and sisters of the great leader are more important than his sons, according to Indian ways. I, the mighty Opechancanough, will inherit over thirty tribes when Wahonsonacock dies."

An old Indian came to the side of the angry *werowance*. A short cloak of skin with the fur attached hung over one shoulder. An otter skin hung from his belt with the tail fastened between his thighs. His hair was cropped short except for a ridge in the middle and front. A tiny blackbird was fastened behind one ear.

The old man leaned downward and whispered something to Opechancanough whose stern face almost smiled. Perhaps the old conjurer had made a wise suggestion: "Learn more about these strangers in our land," he had said.

Calling Navirans to his side, Opechancanough began to give commands.

Then Navirans tried to explain to his English friends

that Opechancanough had invited Captain Newport alone for a banquet and an overnight visit.

But the other Englishmen did not understand that they were not invited. When Captain Newport rose to follow Opechancanough and his guards, John Smith, Gabriel Archer, and the others followed, breastplates clanking noisily.

Opechancanough turned. Wrath and contempt glared from his black eyes. Rage and uncertainty tightened his mouth. Do they understand my invitation? he wondered. Do they dare to distrust me and disobey? Shall I destroy them now, or wait and learn more about them later?

"Go." Opechancanough commanded the Englishmen, and he pointed toward the river.

Navirans dropped his head in shame. He had failed to make his new friends understand the invitation, and he had angered Opechancanough. There was nothing he could do now but lead Captain Newport and the others back to his own village.

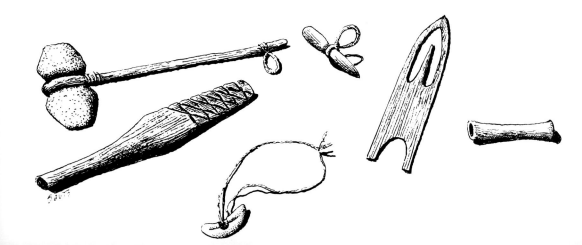

Farewell, Navirans

The shallop drifted soundlessly with the outgoing tide. Discouragement is a quiet companion. Now Captain Newport would have to face his king without news of treasures or trade routes.

At Turkey Isle, a dugout carrying some of Navirans's friends paddled out to meet him. Their boat was filled with clams, mussels and fish. They gave two shouts of welcome and began to talk excitedly.

Navirans answered them in excited tones, too. Suddenly, he dived over the side and climbed into the dugout. With sad eyes he looked back at the Englishmen and gave two shouts of farewell.

Although they begged and promised gifts, Navirans refused to guide them farther. Shaking his head, he asked his Indian friends to give their shellfish to the Englishmen as a parting gift.

Suddenly, the explorers began to feel afraid. There seemed to have been an exchange of news among the Indians. This and Navirans's unexplained farewell made them fear for the colony of Jamestown.

"Sail and oar," commanded Captain Newport.

Branches to Palisades

As the shallop anchored at Jamestown, groans of suffering could be heard. Sentinels were standing watch, and the colonists were aboard the ships.

The colonists explained that, while they were making clapboards, the Paspahegh Indians had attacked. Their stone-tipped arrows and cudgels of stone had been faster than the slow-firing English muskets.

A thick tree limb, shattered by the ship's cannon, had saved the colony. As the limb fell, its branches had struck the attacking warriors. The colonists had run, dragging their wounded onto the ships. Nearly twenty men had been hurt. Now a ship's boy lay dying.

Captain Newport knew that he could not leave the Jamestown colony until the palisaded fort was finished. Tree branch barricades were not enough. President Wingfield agreed. The ragged arrow hole in his beard had convinced him.

Sweating, swearing gentlemen joined the laborers with swinging axes. The salt of their bodies oozed out in the summer heat. Soured, smelly jerkins clung to their wet, hairy chests.

The river water was brackish and slimy at low tide. It did not quench thirst. The marshes swarmed with

needle-nosed mosquitoes. Buzzing and whining, they sucked the Englishmen's blood.

The fort was finished about mid-June. Nearly an acre of land was protected within the wooden triangle. It was 420 feet long on the river side and 300 feet long on the other two sides. The main gate in the long side faced the river. Watchtowers with demi-culverins, or small cannon, were mounted above each gate.

Inside the palisades were huts for sleeping, a storehouse, a guardhouse and a church. Grass thatched roofs were designed to keep out the rain, snow and hail.

"Now King James has a settlement in the New World," the colonists said. But the Paspahegh Indians were not so sure.

The Captain Sails

President Wingfield announced a day of rest after
the fort was finished. Reverend Hunt held the first
Anglican communion service in the new church on
the 21st of June. Captain John Smith described the
church as "a homely thing like a barne . . . covered
with rafts, sedge and earthe."

The two larger ships were loaded with clapboards for
the Virginia Company to sell. The pinnace, *Discovery*,
would be left with the colony.

A locked sea chest in the captain's cabin held letters
for friends and relatives back home. There were also

reports for the Virginia Company of London and King James I. Notes and maps were the only means the colonists had to give England a picture of the New World.

Voices carrying last-minute messages and well-wishes filled the air. "God speed you to return soon," they called.

On June 22, 1607, the *Susan Constant* and *Godspeed* sailed down the James toward the Atlantic Ocean.

Christopher Newport braced himself on the tilting quarterdeck. His left hand shaded his far-seeing eyes. His weather-beaten face felt the warmth of the rising sun.

He faced the future bravely, although he feared for the colony he had left behind. He prayed silently that he would be able to return soon with supplies.

Captain Newport had bade farewell to over one hundred of his countrymen. More than half would die before he returned. Four more round-trip voyages to Jamestown would be his destiny, though this he could not know.

One day his son would inherit Virginia land.

Thereafter

There are many stories about Jamestown after that June day in 1607—tales of shipwreck, attempted mutiny, epidemics and starvation.

There are stories of friendships formed and battles waged with the many Algonquian tribes. One of these stories tells how Powhatan's daughter, Pocahontas, was kidnapped by the colonists to force a ransom of peace. She married John Rolfe and moved to England, never to see Virginia again.

Opechancanough ruled after Wahonsonacock and lived over ninety years. He remained unfriendly to the English and never stopped trying to drive them from his land.

The colonists made further attempts at hunting for gold, a new trade route to the Orient, and the lost colony of Roanoke Island. Defeated in their searching, they finally turned to other tasks.

Their ships returned to England filled with pitch, tar, timber, sassafras and other natural products, but these trading supplies could not support the growing colony. Attempts at glass making and silk raising for export failed as well.

Jamestown prospered for the first time when its

colonists successfully cultivated tobacco, the Indian "weed of peace." In 1613 the first shipment of pressed golden leaves filled the ships for England, and supplies came back in exchange.

Forts and settlements spread up and down the James and its tributaries. English roots grew deeper and deeper into Virginia soil.

And so the land of the Paspahegh Indians became the first permanent English settlement in North America. Jamestown, the birthplace of the nation, remained the capital of the colony for 92 years.

*   *   *

Today Jamestown Island is a national shrine. There, exhibits and artifacts of colonial times can be seen in a Visitor's Center. A Wilderness Road circles through the forest. Pictorial markers along the way tell the settlement story.

Today mist continues to rise from the marshes and curious deer watch from the forest. The spirit of the Jamestown of 1607 seems to be there still, on the small river island in Virginia.

The Jamestown Colonists—1607

CHRISTOPHER NEWPORT—Captain

HENRY ADLING—Gentleman

JEREMY ALICOCK—Gentleman

GABRIEL ARCHER—Captain,
Gentleman

JOHN ASBIE

BENJAMIN BEAST—Gentleman

ROBERT BEHETHLAND—
Gentleman

EDWARD BRINTO—Mason,
Soldier

EDWARD BROOKES—Gentleman
Died in West Indies

JOHN BROOKES—Gentleman

EDWARD BROWNE—Gentleman

JAMES BRUMFIELD—Boy

WILLIAM BRUSTER—
Gentleman

JOHN CAPPER

GEORGE CASSEN—Laborer

THOMAS CASSEN—Laborer

WILLIAM CASSEN—Laborer

EUSTACE CLOVILL—Gentleman

SAMUELL COLLIER—Boy

ROGER COOKE—Gentleman

THOMAS COWPER—Barber

RICHARD CROFTS—Gentleman

RICHARD DIXON—Gentleman

JOHN DODS—Laborer, Soldier

OLD EDWARD—Laborer

THOMAS EMRY—Carpenter

ROBERT FENTON—Gentleman

GEORGE FLOWER—Gentleman

ROBERT FORD—Gentleman

RICHARD FRITH—Gentleman

STEPHEN GALTHORPE

WILLIAM GARRET—Bricklayer

GEORGE GOULDING—Laborer

THOMAS GORE—Gentleman

ANTHONY GOSNOLD—
Gentleman

ANTHONY GOSNOLL—
Gentleman

BARTHOLOMEW GOSNOLD—
Captain, Councilor

THOMAS GOWER—Gentleman

STEPHEN HALTHROP—
Gentleman

EDWARD HARRINGTON—
Gentleman

JOHN HERD—Bricklayer

NICHOLAS HOULGRAVE—
Gentleman

ROBERT HUNT—Master,
Preacher, Gentleman

THOMAS JACOB—Sergeant

WILLIAM JOHNSON—Laborer

GEORGE KENDALL—Captain, Councilor

ELLIS KINGSTON—Gentleman

WILLIAM LAXON—Carpenter

JOHN LAYDON—Laborer

WILLIAM LOVE—Tailor

JOHN MARTIN—Captain, Councilor

JOHN MARTIN—Gentleman

GEORGE MARTIN—Gentleman

FRANCIS MIDWINTER—Gentleman

EDWARD MORISH—Gentleman, Corporal

THOMAS MOUNSLIC

THOMAS MOUTON

RICHARD MUTTON—Boy

NATHANIEL PECOCK—Boy, Soldier

JOHN PENNINGTON—Gentleman

GEORGE PERCY—Master, Gentleman

DRU PICKHOUSE—Gentleman

EDWARD PISING—Carpenter

NATHANIELL POWELL—Gentleman

JONAS PROFIT—Sailor

JOHN RATCLIFFE—Captain, Councilor

JAMES READ—Blacksmith

JEHU ROBINSON—Gentleman

WILLIAM RODS—Laborer

THOMAS SANDS—Gentleman

JOHN SHORT—Gentleman

RICHARD SIMONS—Gentleman

NICHOLAS SKOT—Drummer

ROBERT SMALL—Carpenter

WILLIAM SMETHES—Gentleman

JOHN SMITH—Captain, Councilor

FRANCIS SNARSBROUGH—Gentleman

JOHN STEVENSON—Gentleman

THOMAS STUDLEY—Gentleman

WILLIAM TANKARD—Gentleman

HENRY TAVIN—Laborer

KELLAM THROGMORTON—Gentleman

ANAS TODKILL—Soldier

WILLIAM UNGER—Laborer

JOHN WALLER—Gentleman

GEORGE WALKER—Gentleman

THOMAS WEBBE—Gentleman

WILLIAM WHITE—Laborer

WILLIAM WILKINSON—Surgeon

EDWARD MARIA WINGFIELD—Master, Councilor, President

THOMAS WOTTON—Gentleman, Surgeon

"with diverse others."

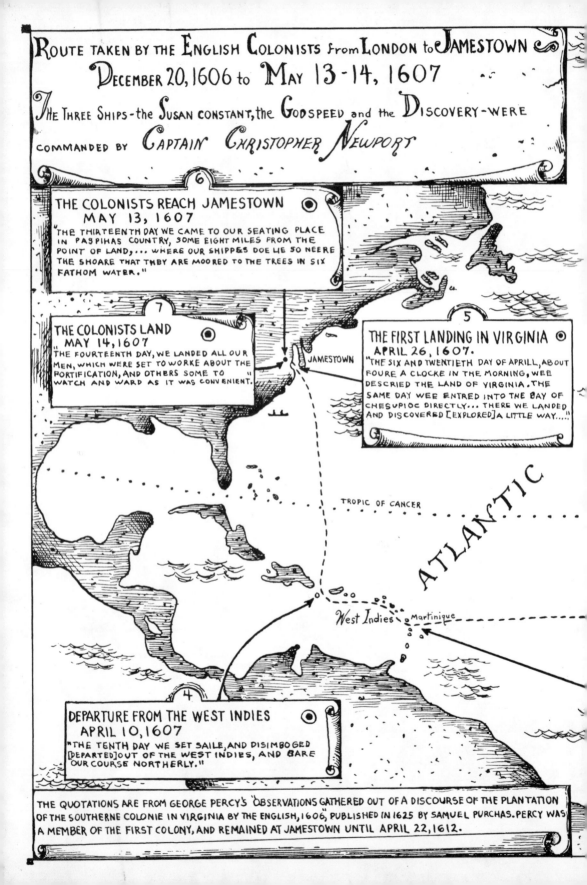